START UP STRATEGY

How to Start the Startup of Your Dream and

Strategies

(Startup Evolution Curve From Idea to Profitable

and Scalable Business)

Dolores Hawk

Published By Andrew Zen

Dolores Hawk

Start Up Strategy: How to Start the Startup of Your Dream and Strategies (Startup Evolution Curve From Idea to Profitable and Scalable Business)

ISBN 978-1-77485-258-3

Legal & Disclaimer

The information contained in this book is not designed to replace or take the place of any form of medicine or professional medical advice. The information in this book has been provided for educational and entertainment purposes only.

The information contained in this book has been compiled from sources deemed reliable, and it is accurate to the best of the Author's knowledge; however, the Author cannot guarantee its accuracy and validity and cannot be held liable for any errors or omissions. Changes are periodically made to this book. You must consult your doctor or get professional medical advice before using any of the suggested remedies, techniques, or information in this book.

Upon using the information contained in this book, you agree to hold harmless the Author from and against any damages, costs, and expenses, including any legal fees potentially resulting from the application of any of the information provided by this guide. This disclaimer applies to any damages or injury caused by the use and application, whether directly or indirectly, of any advice or information presented, whether for breach of contract, tort, negligence, personal injury, criminal intent, or under any other cause of action.

You agree to accept all risks of using the information presented inside this book. You need to consult a professional medical practitioner in order to ensure you are both able and healthy enough to participate in this program.

TABLE OF CONTENTS

Introduction

In this book, we'll provide everything you need to be aware of about coaching online.

Many online coaches do their job incorrectly. They chase their clients. They attempt to offer coaching services for a low price. If they do this, they don't have any control over their clients and have poor retention rates in the coaching program they offer.

This book will teach you how to stay clear of these mistakes and start an effective coaching business.

If you're looking to become an online coach who is successful You must think about and approach this business in a certain manner. You must be able to draw clients rather than trying to chase them. You'd like to attract clients who do exactly what you ask you to expect them to. You should charge high rates and not have clients who try to nickel and dime you.

To achieve this, you must consider thinking in a particular manner and approach the business of online coaching in a particular manner.

This book will begin by discussing the differentiators between the business of coaching online and a career as coach. Then, we will discuss what you must consider about earning a decent income by becoming an online instructor.

Each of the successful online coaches is well-known for certain things. They are renowned for a particular kind of name and. The process of building a reputation from the ground up is what we'll discuss in the coming weeks.

Coaching online isn't just providing guidance. It's about exerting control over your clients, and making sure they are satisfied and receiving value according to how they see value. We will discuss all this in the chapter entitled "What you are selling in your role as an online coach isn't what clients buy."

We will also cover the issues of avoiding mistakes and of receiving a payment.

The knowledge you discover in this book can be applied in any industry and has any size of company.

It's a great option if you're a health coach who works in a private setting with customers one-on one. This is also an option if are looking to coach entrepreneurs or freelancers who employ a small number of people for their company. It is also possible to apply the strategies and advice from the book when working with large companies.

The first thing you must know about b2b, also known as business-to-business selling is that there isn't such thing. Businesses do not purchase everything. People buy everything.

If you're selling to consumers, the customers generally have one question regarding your product or services: "Is this for me?" They may wonder about price, alternatives, and other questions however they're trying to determine what products or services are suitable for consumers.

Selling to business is more complex. Business buyers are looking to find two different questions. The first is like the one for consumers:

Is this for my business?

Business buyers usually have another concern. They are also trying to determine what they stand to gain from this transaction. A product or service might be an ideal match for their company however, within the company, they are unable to decide on a purchase right now. This is similar to

If my company buys it, is this beneficial to me personally?

This is what it is. In selling directly to the consumer, there is a major issue for businesses selling to consumers. you have two options.

The rest is exactly the same.

When you sell to businesses it is still selling to customers who have emotions and have feelings. They also make decisions the same way that your clients do. The numbers can change. The principles and strategies don't.

What you'll often think after studying this work is: "This sounds great, however, my business is unique. It might work for a coach working in X however it will not be a good fit for me."

These thoughts are not beneficial. It's always self-sabotage.

The search for reasons that something doesn't be successful or doesn't work isn't an extremely lucrative job.

Every janitor, taxi driver, McDonald's employee, or low-wage worker could find reasons as to that they're not working in a job pay a good amount. Making excuses isn't difficult.

What's harder, and the most important to wealth and prosperity is understanding what it means for you, your circumstances and your company. This is what you've always wanted to be doing.

It is also important to eliminate the notion that you must have an academic degree or qualification from a particular institution in order to be an effective online coach.

Do you know the place you can find out where Dr. Phil went to school? What is the story with Tony Robbins? What do you think of Gary Vaynerchuk or Grant Cordone?

Most likely, you aren't. The truth is that the market does not care. The formal requirements are all blocks you've got within your mind. They're not the actual blocks for success as an online coach.

Chapter 1: The Startup Entrepreneur

If you're a business owner, you're also an Entrepreneur. Entrepreneurs are those who manage or are in charge of a company's operations. Entrepreneurs in the startup phase are creative business owners who usually take advantage of emerging trends and opportunities which allows them to offer something unique to the world or present the same thing in a different way. They also are willing to risk their lives. Their primary goal is to make as much as their abilities permit.

Me? An Entrepreneur?

There is no requirement for an undergraduate degree or specific training to become an entrepreneur who is a startup. Actually there are many well-known and successful businessmen have dropped out of college (although I don't recommend such a thing!). The examples of people such as Andrew Carnegie and Mark Ecko proves that anyone is able to be an entrepreneur. All you need is require the drive and determination to succeed.

You're an entrepreneur at heart? If you're not sure you are, then there's no reason to fret. Certain individuals are better at being entrepreneurs however anyone who would like to become an entrepreneur!

The Habits of a Startup Entrepreneur

Here are some of the traits that are typically found in entrepreneurs:

You're an active imaginative, insatiable mind that is constantly making and thinking. You are always thinking of and exploring new ideas , and new ways to do things.

You have big dreams and are determined to do anything to bring those dreams reality.

It is easy to spot an untrue idea once you come across one.

You are always thinking how you could make your life better, and you always would like to help others.

You would like to be a good person.

You're a disciplined person.

You don't enjoy taking instructions from others. You'd prefer to take the driving seat.

Reflect on your experience and search for "lessons learned" to help you improve your performance.

You're naturally curious about learning about new things and gaining new perspectives on what you already are familiar with.

You like getting up early to start your day to accomplish more. are more likely to fall asleep at the same time each evening.

You're particularly interested in understanding how companies operate, and you'd like to know more about their internal workings.

You're not dissuaded by constructive criticism, you're open and sensitive to feedback.

You are able to overcome adversity and don't let any obstacle or hurdle hinder you from your goal. You recognize the importance and reward for your hard work. You always seek out new opportunities.

You are able to discern your strengths and are aware of and accept your weaknesses.

You love making goals and making daily routines. You establish a timeframe to accomplish each goal that you are striving to achieve.

It is important to exercise regularly and follow the right diet to keep your body and mind in top shape, to enable you to perform at a high level.

You are willing to take risks and are not scared to meet strangers.

You're highly disciplined with your time management abilities. Others are able to set their watch with your help.

Do not let failure stop you or hinder your progress. You're determined to see your goals come true regardless of whatever challenges you face.

Ask the appropriate questions, ones that can help you succeed.

You're a planner. You always need plans for the day.

You're a delegator. know the best people and you trust them to assist in your strategy.

You're a competitorand you'd prefer to be ahead.

You can tell "no" to things that you're not comfortable with or to things you consider to be a wasted time.

You can spot the potential of other people and you can aid them in becoming successful.

You are respectful of others regardless of their character or culture.

You're confident about your abilities and capabilities.

You remain calm even in difficult circumstances and you are able to make decisions that are based on facts and logic instead of emotions.

A Startup Defined

A startup business is one that is new and small, but it has the potential to be extremely profitable. Entrepreneurs who start a startup typically launch businesses with the aim of offering a novel solution or product that will assist others, no matter the amount - or how small - revenue it can produce. Most often, a new business is only around for a couple of years before it starts to earn a name for itself or even make profits. The goal of a businessman who is a startup may not be initially to earn lots of money but a startup entrepreneur generally has a plan for their business idea eventually gaining the upper hand in the market.

A business that is new is typically considered to be a startup for the initial 3 to 5 years or until it joins with a larger business, expands to another location, adds over 75 workers or has earned a significant revenue.

Chapter 2: Researching Your

Audience

In the preceding chapter, you were taught how to research firms and their partners within the companies. Being aware of both of these aspects let you know which companies and partners are the best to collaborate with to ensure you benefit the most from your financing deal. Once you've been well-informed about these two types of platforms, we'll continue to be attentive to specific aspects: partners.

When it comes time to make an application to receive money through a venture capitalist company it is crucial to know who you are pitching to. After you've screened potential partners to determine those who could be the greatest for your company and your business, it's time you go further. It is essential to be certain of who your people you choose to partner with, the qualities they are looking for, what you have to look at as well as what they're prepared to offer your business. You will find out more about how they've completed previous deals as well as what others say about them, and what they can benefit you. This will allow you to identify the people you'd like to collaborate with the most and the best way to craft your pitch to ensure it will succeed. If you're ready clarify the people you want to reach Let's start looking at the details!

What is their belief system?

Like you like to examine your mission statements for the venture capital firm and vice versa, it is also important to take a look at the goals or mission statements of the partner. In most cases, you can get this through asking questions or searching online.

If you are planning to enter into business with a partner you must know what beliefs they hold. This will provide you with an overview of the extent to which their beliefs are compatible with your own in business. Additionally, it can aid in determining whether their beliefs are in line with your business's beliefs as well. It is important to ensure that you choose someone who shares similar objectives for you. Although their primary objective is to earn back funds from their investment in venture capital but their second objective should be helping you to push your business towards success. Anyone who is successful in venture capital will recognize that their help and advice is essential but the company's founder is the one who has the vision and dream, and, ultimately, the one who will propel the company towards the top.

Ideally, you'd like someone who is an active involvement, yet who does not interfere with your involvement and you. The partner shouldn't be afraid to provide their opinion and help get where you need to be, but they shouldn't come in to mow you down to take control. You need someone who views you as an equalpartner, acknowledge your contributions into the equation, and wants to complement your strengths in a manner that will help you both bring your company up to where it should take it. If you work together efficiently, your company will become the dream business and the venture capitalist is more likely to come out investing in a business which is highly profitable and bring the amount they invested in the first place and is seeking to return.

Alongside knowing how your partners will collaborate in conjunction with your company Knowing what their values are ahead of time can give you an edge when you present the idea. The reason is you must present your concept in a manner that is appealing to their values and the things they are interested in. If your business's idea is compatible with their mission statement, and you can demonstrate that you have the same or similar values regarding business, the objective of your company and the direction you intend to take it You are more likely to attract the attention of their audience and keep their curiosity before getting to the actual presentation portion in your pitch. In a way, knowing the beliefs of your audience and their your own mission statement, you can customize your presentation to attract the areas they are interested and what they value. This means that they'll be more likely to be curious about your message and want to be involved with you.

What's their reputation?

It is crucial to understand is the name of the capitalist is prior to deciding to go into the business of them. Knowing whom the person is who they are, their track record is, what others are saying about them and how they present themselves when they are in the presence of other people is a good method to gain a solid concept of the person you are as well as what they're seeking. This will help you in a variety different ways that knowing their beliefs.

In the beginning, if you know what your person's track record is you'll be able to determine with certainty of whether you'd like to collaborate with them. In the case of a partner whose reputation is sour and they're well-known as unfriendly, pushy, or overbearing, and they do not have the best outcomes from the ventures they pursue in the past, then you don't prefer working with them. Although the failings could be a coincidence, they could be directly related to the reputation of the partner and their inability to collaborate with other business people in the world. As bad is when you hire someone who acts as a wet noodle when it comes to business. This is someone who is willing to put up money and offer their opinions, but never give you any guidance or knowledge to help you progress or achieve greater results for your venture. It is important to ensure that you're hiring someone with a great reputation, who is known for using a heavy hand in a manner that produces results. It is important to choose one who will be part of your team, and who can ensure that the team will succeed and help in the process of getting there. The partner you select should be determined to be a part of your company, believes in the work they support and is able to provide you with a variety of opportunities for networking and connections to expand your business.

If you're looking at someone's reputation you are able to gain an understanding of the way they worked with other people. It is vital that, when you examine the reputation of someone, you're willing to examine it on a variety of different levels. If you look at someone's reputation solely from one point of view (the perspective of unsuccessful business ventures for instance) can provide you with an extremely biased view of the person. People who offer their opinions could be smug or angry about the fact that their efforts didn't succeed and are therefore trying to blame others instead of taking responsibility for their actions. It is crucial to examine the various people who have been in contact with the partner. Check out their venture capital investment, their other investments and business partnerships and also who they are known as generally. Find out the extent of your reputation in order you know whether or not the negative media coverage is caused by someone trying at blaming them for an transaction that went wrong, or if they actually have a reputation as difficult to deal with or difficult to work with to work with in business.

When you've come familiar with their reputation and you've found some you're attracted to and want to work with, you have the chance to use this advantage to your advantage. Again, take advantage of their name as a way to customize your message to the partner you wish to appeal to. If, for instance, you're presenting to a client who has been known as an aggressive and go-getter in business, demonstrate the way your business is founded on that go-getter mindset and also how you are able to demonstrate this type of attitude. Also, demonstrate the company why it needs this kind of mindset to move forward in ways you can't take on yourself to drive the company forward. Let them know how your personalities compliment each other and how this can benefit the success of the business you manage.

If you can take a look at the person who you're giving your presentation to and have a fair idea of who they are, what they can bring to your company and also how you can help the person, preparing your presentation much more straightforward. If you are able to understand someone's beliefs as well as their personality or reputation It becomes much simpler to make them feel welcome to your business in a way that they are more open. If you're pitching in a manner that doesn't reflect the person they are as a person, their style of living or their values the chances of being taken on as an investor decrease significantly.

What is their special area of Specialization?

Understanding a person's specific field of expertise is extremely vital. There are a variety of reasons you should learn about the partner's specialization. For instance, if are seeking to break into the finance industry, but are pitching an individual who has more experience in the retail sector and you are unable to secure an investment proposal. This is due to the fact that many venture capitalists be hesitant to go with the information they have in order to avoid a bad deal. Additionally, you wouldn't think of working with someone who has little or no experience in your field, as this could lead to you working with someone who's not beneficial to your business. If you're both in the same boat, this might not be the most beneficial one.

If you end in negotiating a deal with someone beyond your area of expertise, you may find yourself caught in a situation in which you are partnered with someone who's trying to gauge in the area of expertise, however this isn't relevant to the field you work in. For instance, they could look to make comparisons between apples and oranges in retail and finance in order to ensure that business transactions work to their advantage. Since their only experience they possess is that of finance, this is the place they could offer suggestions. It's not necessarily relevant or even helpful to retailers however. However, since they hold the largest share of the board of directors, they might be able use their influence to force you to make bad business decisions and dealings with your business. Although you may think this won't occur however, the reality is it might happen, and the result could be disastrous for your business.

You should instead search for opportunities to acquire partners who are experienced in the field you are working in. It is important to find partners who have already been doing business in the sector or field you're in, and who have at least one instance of results over time. The more they understand about your company and what they are up to, the easier it is for them to assist you and assist in being successful in your business. It is important to ensure that you have someone who will guide you, offer you suggestions and help you when you need help, and can be an effective and positive representative in your Board of Directors for many years to be.

If you're considering your partners and pondering which ones will be the best partner for your business take a look at the business you run specifically. What is your industry? What are your customers? What is your target audience? Which audience do you appear to be most open from? Choose a partner who appears to be a good fit for these characteristics as well. For instance, if you're in a market which is dominated by middle-aged women, selecting someone younger with a lot of experience serving younger men might not be beneficial for you. They might not have a solid concept of what your market is, and how best to assist them, which can result in you not being able to reach your intended market. Instead, look for someone with an in-depth comprehension of your market as well as your business and the purpose you have. Although you might not find an individual who is perfect for the above categories The closer you reach a perfect match the more effective. It is important to ensure that the person who you are placing on the board of directors an asset and not one who is a liability.

What is their track record?

Then, look at the history of the person you're looking to form into a partnership. What has their track record been to date? What has they achieved successfully and what did they not? Are they having any major achievements to their credit? Have they had any achievements even? For how long are they in the business? For how long has they served as venture capitalist?

Examining someone's history and asking these questions is an effective method of ensuring your choice of who you team up with isn't going to fail you right from the beginning. Like the partner has to be screened thoroughly by the business and you to ensure that you're going to be a successful business decision to them, you too should thoroughly review your partner and ensure that they'll be an excellent business partner for you. Discovering their previous business experience and determining where you've had success as well as when you've seen failure is an excellent way to get a sense of the person they are and the things they have achieved. Be aware of the areas of the business they have succeeded in, particularly. If, for instance, you're looking for one who is a master in their industry, but seems to have greater success in different areas that are not related to yours You might want to look into this. If you discover someone else with greater success in the field you are in and you are able to choose to select that person over the one who is more successful in a different area. Although this might seem insignificant or irrelevant but when it comes to running your business , you need the most reliable people behind your business. Someone who has proven their success in your particular field or area over everyone else's is an excellent way to ensure that you're maximizing your profits as well as getting the best benefit of your collaboration.

Additionally, if you look at someone's past and notice that they've never been able to record any wins or successes over the past few years, and they are doing it for quite a while it is possible to look into the reason this happens. Be aware that the majority of venture capital deals are not successful and it often is due to the fact that not every company is designed to run smoothly from the beginning. But, if almost all of the ventures are an unfavorable experience for the partner, it might make you wonder whether they had something to do with the reason the reason why no previous ventures have been successful. You can research some of the companies they've invested in and see if it is possible to find out anything about the company and the role that they had in creation to the direction the company is now. This could help you gain some idea as to whether they're reliable and also if they're profitable, in the first place.

In addition to examining their history in venture capital deals examine their history in business generally. Have they entered into any other agreements or partnerships other than venture capital which have been successful? Are they renowned for business ventures which are a big success? Do they personally have any companies of their own? Find out more about not just their experience with venture capital, but also their overall business background all around. If they appear to be successful or have at the very least, some really impressive achievements, they could be worth partnering with. But if it appears that the majority of their work fails and they're not well-known for anything this could be more risky than your business could afford to take.

The Verdict

After having done all of the above research about the potential partners after which you are able to go on and make your own decision on them. Here is where you take a look at the results of what you've learned and begin to determine which partners you'd be interested in partnering with based on how the partnership will likely succeed, and which partners you're least enthusiastic about. In this instance, you are able to consider them on three levels: the ones you would like the most as well as those that you'd prefer if the partners you were most interested in didn't meet your expectations, and the ones that you won't choose to partner with. Even if they appear to be great initially but after doing some research, you might find out that they're not the person they're made out to be and you should stay clear of them. It's completely normal. You should keep these names on your list or remember them to prevent you of conducting any business. A deal that isn't worth it is one that is sure to bring you down or turn sour in the beginning.

After you've created your lists of the people you would like to work with and those who you would prefer to work with, if these were not accessible to you then you should begin thinking about the best way to present your presentation! This is where you'll be able to let your business shine, so that you can present a message that impresses your audience . Hopefully, it will land you the job that you've always wanted So don't be afraid to create a memorable one. If you're eager to master the art of presentation proceed into Chapter 3, Creating Your Presentationtoday.

Chapter 3: Innovation Bending

A common misconception among those who are looking to establish an enterprise is that they they must develop an innovative, revolutionary idea that can transform the world. Sure, it would be the ideal scenario and everyone wants to come up with something that anyone can profit from. But this type of thinking usually creates an untrue excuse that we think is a reason not to begin a business simply because we couldn't come up with the most unique idea. In addition, the greater your originality it is the greater risk you're taking (this could also translate into greater potential profits should you are successful). This is due to the fact that totally new way of doing things has not been tested and even with thorough market research, it's difficult to determine how people will react to unique offerings or even services. Remember that a thought that seems to be a bad idea could be better than an enticing idea when it is properly executed of a business model by taking actions. The idea might seem amazing when you first come up with it, but you could discover that you have to make many adjustments to it to ensure that people will appreciate the product or service. It's true that you don't know until you test after you've accomplished everything you could in the beginning stages of analysis and the building of your business.

In the end, if you haven't found that original concept (a very difficult job) of your desires don't fret. There are plenty of concepts you could come up with to improve your business's performance by cleverly and ingenuously adjusting (or upgrading) existing products, ideas or services.

While you're improving the ideas you have Here are some suggestions to think about.

Respond to the need

What needs are you seeking to meet? Let's discuss what people really need. Needs differ from desires and can be described as the requirements that individuals be able to perform their duties in a normal and productive the modern world.

The requirements to survive may include:

Food: We all need to consume food. This may seem obvious, but it is an area that is huge enough to come up with a lot of ideas for. Because people need food and eat, food businesses are thriving in comparison to other industries, even during times of economic downturn. You can come up with new concepts to serve customers directly, such as tasty recipes for catering truck, or a bar or restaurant with intriguing themes.

Here's a list examples of this:

http://www.thrillist.com/drink/nation/21-best-theme-bars-in-america-thrillist-nation

My personal favorite is Kalamazoo Bar Exchange, which is listed on this list. This bar has drinks prices fluctuate based on the demand and what the bar wants to sell in the present. There will be occasions where you come up with ideas and conduct research that you'll wish you'd thought of an idea prior to putting it into practice. This is the concept I'd like to have thought of because I am a huge fan of food, drinks and trading. It would have been ideal.

If you do experience this feeling, don't fret because there are many ideas that you could come up with and, as I said before, you are always able to enhance your ideas to be competitive against your competitors in business. If you can provide customers what they want and appreciate, you've started your business with a solid foundation. In the case of the food industry you are aware that people search for food. Many people prefer to dine out, so you're not creating a new sector or sub-sector completely from the ground up.

You can also come up with ideas for catering companies that be a direct impact on the final user, who are people who come to the establishment for food. It could be kitchen equipment that can allow individuals to peel items faster and with greater efficiency (things that can save chefs time) or a fridge that has been designed to be cleverly so that it can accommodate more food items while making it easy to access.

Shelter: Everybody needs an area to be able to live in. This is a huge area to think of ideas for. It could include anything starting with basic materials for the construction industry, to furniture, construction appliances, and so on. Consider the fundamental necessity for shelter, and consider ways you can enhance the quality of life for consumers on a daily basis. You can also enter the real estate industry and purchase as well as sell homes (houses and condos, villas that have the pool and the nice things).

You can also opt for a different method and tackle the issue from a different angle. 3-D printing houses are amazing and was one of the innovations that made me incredibly exuberant in my career as an engineer.

The World's First 3D-printed Apartment Building constructed in China

http://www.cnet.com/uk/news/worlds-first-3d-printed-apartment-building-constructed-in-china/

I personally want to renovate and sell homes as I am able to save. I am aware that this isn't an original idea, however, as I mentioned earlier, you shouldn't stand in the dark because you don't have a unique idea, and that everyone does what they would like to do. When you begin to gain more experience in your business, new ideas will be able to hit you.

If you truly want to pursue something, but you are unsure, start by taking the first step. Even if you are unable to start an enterprise that is related to your interest, take on an opportunity to find out more about the subject. So long as you make a decision to take action and don't give up on your goals and goals, you're on the right path as an entrepreneurial. You'll notice that as you work through the problems you face that you are more open to new ideas and you will be able discern what other people are not doing.

Water: Who says they don't have water? Water is the only thing that can be lived without. In the report of UN WATER coordinated by UNESCO 780 million people have no access to safe water and 2.3 billion suffer from inadequate sanitation. Even in the more developed nations water is a resource which must be utilized with care. There are a lot of ideas that can be developed to tackle this. If you are able to come up with useful solutions, but do not have the resourcesto implement them, you can get the patent to your idea and sell it to someone who is able to implement it.

To meet this essential requirement, think of ways to make it easier to access water. Consider, for instance, ways to reduce costs. A compact and cost-effective device that could purify seawater might serve this function.

I discovered this water bottle that is reusable on Kickstarter that is green and supports an important goal.

https://www.kickstarter.com/projects/699920953/nada-bottle-collapsible-water-bottle-clean-water?ref=category

Large corporations and government agencies have control over this market, so it is difficult to join, but If you're creative, you could find ways to market your concept or a prototype , and earn profits from it. It is also possible to create items or products that complement this market.

Naturally, it is possible to create new drinks, but bear in mind that you are subject to lots of regulation due to its direct effect on the health of people.

Fill the need

There are many items and services that can improve the quality of life, but do not affect the life of an individual. However, this doesn't suggest that they are not necessary however, since the deficiency of a few of these aspects could result in physical harm or emotional stress. There are also products that consumers don't even think they would like. Through effective advertising it is possible to get the desired response created for these products.

Entertainment and Recreation It is possible to come up with suggestions for any service or product that will allow people to be entertained. Consumers can choose from a range of interests and prefer to pursue what they love. Examples of entertainment or recreation could include bungee-jumping or managing the bowling alley, offering podcasts, etc.

Beauty: When you put the simple sanitary necessities like brushing your teeth or showering aside, our modern lifestyle is very demanding when it comes to appearance. It is unlikely that we will be able to live if we don't have a haircut every day and yet maintaining your appearance is both safe and pleasing to the eye for ourselves and to others' perception of our appearance. Examples of this include perfume, clothing and other items.

Socialization It is an vital need for you to create a myriad of ideas. People need to socialize and interact with other people to make living life more. When it comes to services, mobile phone marketplaces are filled with apps which make it easier to connect with strangers, particularly for relationships.

Career Development: Who does not want to have a career path that will allow them to improve their skills? If you have a lot of experience in an field that is related to careers You can provide online classes and write books or create a career counseling service. Don't just cater to people working full-time for companies. The fields of management and entrepreneurship are two professions that can help entrepreneurs or managers to become more effective in their work.

The rest of the information can be found here. You could imagine a totally different product that consumers aren't familiar with. It is possible to bring attention for your product via social media as well as other strategies like paid newspaper ads or billboards. If you can make your advertising effective it is possible to make "the desire".

Innovation Bending Step-by-Step

There's another term , 'patent bending' which is only applicable to patents. You may be in awe of ideas already available on the marketplace or you'll discover that what you've thought of is already in existence and that someone has been selling it for some time. Some of these items or services might not be patented, hence I refer to it as 'innovation bent' instead of patent bend'.

Let's discuss how to approach an innovation process step-by-step.

Step 1: Select one Sector

The first step is to choose the industry you wish to target. In addition, you should decide if you want to provide either a product or service.

Step 2: Conduct In-Depth Research

Learn everything about the subject in question. Find out what kinds of products or services are available and in what ways specific aspects of these companies will enhance your concept. Do you have a way that you could integrate certain ideas from these into your own? Perhaps there is a purpose of the product you plan to provide which you can look into including.

Apart from simply Google-ing the name of a service or product and checking it regularly, you can check crowdfunding websites and find out what others are up to.

Here are the top websites:

Kickstarter

Indiegogo

Gofundme

Kickstarter is a great site to look into for projects that are creative since they don't permit funding for personal expenses. For projects that are based on ideas this is my preferred website to explore because it has a vast range of creative and beautiful ideas that you can explore. The more you study these ideas, the more imaginative you'll feel and help you to think of amazing ideas.

Other sources that the internet include catalogs of products (very helpful as you discover a variety of similar products in one source) radio, newspapers, TV shows that focus on inventions and inventions, etc. Everything you read or see can help you expand your horizons and help you come up with ideas.

Step 3: Refine your concept into the your final stage

You should now have a clear idea of what to do. You've conducted your research and analyzed what's out there. Now , you can refine your concept from your research. These are the most important questions to ask yourself and discuss with your business partners , if there are any

What can you do to increase the demographics of the final user?

What are you able to do to improve the quality of the product or the service more user-friendly?

What can you do to make your product more appealing to the eye or make the service more enjoyable?

What is unique in your concept and what is the same? What can you do to turn something like something that is similar to something unique?

How can you cut production costs while maintaining the quality acceptable levels?

Does your service or product meet the requirements of any regulations, If there are any?

Are there any patents on your idea? If so what can you do to modify your idea to ensure that you don't need permission to market it? If you're really keen to pursue your idea, do you want to pay for the patent?

Other considerations to make include:

It is possible to make things bigger or smaller, lighter or heavier more efficient and quicker Chairs or tables that are lighter that are able to be moved easily.

Modifying their material, color, or shape. For instance testing solar panels' color or material or shape.

Modifying the quality of or quantity Batched items can be sold lower prices. You may also improve or decrease the quality of your product to boost profits.

However, regardless of what you do, be sure to keep your customers happy.

Access, mobility and portability. Disposability Portable camping gear that is able to be transported around, a portable coffee maker and disposable cameras.

Making repairs or replacement, maintenance, cleaning: If you have parts of an electronic product that has a limited life-cycle ensure that the part is readily accessible for maintenance or repair. For instance, for items that require frequent replacement of filters ensure that the filter is accessible so that customers can replace it on their own when needed instead of calling your service department to make the change.

Introduce machines, simplifying and convenience: Utilize automated machines during production for accuracy, reducing the number of components inside electronic devices and the Swiss Knives (they are extremely convenient) and many more.

The addition of new products, accessories, or features Find ways to enhance existing products.

Here's an example of how this could be accomplished:

https://www.kickstarter.com/projects/combocases/full-grain-leather-slim-wallet-case-for-iphone-6-a?ref=category

I am a fan of this project since it's a perfect complement to the well-known iPhone 6. It's it's an iPhone case, but it integrates the functions of a wallet in the case. This is a great illustration of an accessory that provides an innovative feature.

Modifying the method of delivery packaging, size/shape of unit such as nicotine patches or pills recyclable or environmentally friendly packaging as well as smaller medical ventilators that could be used for military purposes (increase the portability of units by reducing their size) and so on.

Enhancing usability, performance or safetyby using rechargeable batteries, long-life batteries and an app that minimizes the radiation of a computer screen to minimize the long-term negative effects of continuous use.

Step 4: Determine whether the concept is patentable or is legally permitted for sale

This brings us to greater detail regarding the intellectual property aspect of your concept. Visit UNITED STATES PATENT and TRADEMARK OFFICE to begin searching to find your concept.

Once you have logged on to the website, open with an advanced search. The first step is to conduct a broad search that includes fewer than two keywords (2 keywords recommended). This is because there could be ideas that you overlook that could be relevant to your idea in the event that you perform a specific search initially.

Review the results to see whether there are any similar designs like yours. It could take a lot of time, but it's worthwhile. After you've realized the originality of your idea, do a specific search and search for patents with similar ideas in the future.

Alternately, you could make use of an experienced patent attorney and patent finder. If you are a beginner, this may be a great option since it's usually not easy to determine to know what you should search for. A patent attorney can tell you in detail whether your idea is patentable and the best way you can alter your ideas to ensure that you still receive the patent.

Step 5: Create your own business or organization and implement your idea

It's time to make it real. You may choose to protect the invention. Patenting an idea is absolutely nothing to getting market share until you can actually market it. Patenting an idea, however, has two advantages:

You are the owner of the idea, therefore it is possible to directly market the patent to an individual or entityshould you decide not to pursue your concept due to reasons that are different from one another.

If you are aware of the idea that you have and your competition attempts to exploit the same design or the competitive advantages that your patent provides then you have the right to sue them, effectively securing the rights of your product. This is obviously not the best option and could be expensive. The key thing is to gain a significant part of the market and establish a solid position as a company. In this way, competitors will have a tough time copying what you've done. It is also possible to agree with your competitors by requesting compensation and granting them rights in the event that you choose to not go into a legal fight.

Step 6 Continuous Improvement and Competition

When you've begun selling your product, it's definitely not done. It is a continual process, and you'll face plenty of challenges once you have started selling your product. It is essential to always be looking for competitors and strive to provide the most beneficial product or service to customers. Based on how competitive your competitors are, you'll require investment in research and development, and refine your ideas, while trying to increase your competitive edge. This is especially important for tech firms that frequently seek patents in order in order to maintain their positions in their field.

Innovations are at risk because of the risks

The sale of a product that infringes another's intellectual property could get you into trouble

Patents can be expensive and time-consuming. But you must still think about the possibility. Remember that, in the context of business, gaining a share in the marketplace is far more important than the patent. You could even apply for the patent simultaneously. This means that you could create the product and then apply for the patent simultaneously. So long as the patent is in process, others can't copy your ideas. Instead of sitting around waiting to see the patent granted it is possible to have an audience before approval.

Chapter 4: What Does To Be A

Successful Modern Entrepreneur

"It is the one who is patiently moving step by step...who is certain to be successful to the maximum extent."

The 21st century is witnessing the rising of ever more profitable online entrepreneurs. This is a difficult time for the economy, with increasing numbers of people being laid off, and the possibility of recession becoming more threatening.

In this kind of situation, a significant portion of people will become attracted to entrepreneurship instead of relying solely on the ad-hoc career market.

To become an entrepreneur who is successful in current times, it's not an easy task. You require lots of work and a well-planned approach. Here are some tips which are essential for entrepreneurs of today to succeed:

Be Passionate

If you have a plan that you want to pursue, you have to be prepared to devote most of your daily hours for it. The obstacles may get up but once you've decided you will have to stay true to your goals. You need to be driven to be successful and inspire the group you will begin to form.

Work and be a hard worker

It's been a long time since the past; things have become more efficient and efficient, but there's still a need for working hard. It takes a significant amount of time for any company to succeed and there's lots of hard work and sweat required to achieve it. Luck can be in the favor of those who work hard and are focused on their objectives.

Focus on one direction only

It's never recommended to be in several fields of interest. Your focus will lose focus and the chances of failing are higher when your thoughts are wandering around in a multitude of places. Instead, select a single goal, and then focus on the goal with a laser-like concentration. Once you've established an zone of operation, you can develop a system of automation, or work on another goal or subject.

Find a mentor, if you can.

Many of the successful entrepreneurs of this time were mentored who has already talked the walk. Mentors can impart invaluable insights, knowledge and experiences from real life that can help you learn a lot and often prevent the most common mistakes in business that be made at the beginning. My grandfather John Thomas would say "to be intelligent is to be able learning from mistakes. To be smart is to learn from other people."

Take into consideration the importance of any coach for the player? Would the environment look as if everyone could do it all on their own? Particularly when they're ready to achieve the highest level of success. Another reason is the support which are available with someone who has built up credibility, relationships and connections.

Network a lot

Entrepreneurs and businesses of the present depend heavily on their personal and professional connections to get business. When you build relationships over time, you'll be able to meet other newcomers as well as established professionals within your field.

It is possible to learn about the latest trends in your field and get advice from experienced entrepreneurs. It is also advisable to meet people outside of your field of expertise. You do not know when a business opportunity could be waiting to be discovered.

Do you have an internet presence?

We are living in an digital age, where everyone with access to a PC spends some time browsing the internet. Each business, no matter if it's an established company or multinational company, must have an active presence on the internet. A lot of businesses are succeeding mostly due to their online marketing strategies.

After the intricacies of your company are sorted out and you have a solid structure in place, create an optimized website, with all of the pertinent details and contact information. If your business is appealing to the younger crowd You can set up an account for your business on social media site and create awareness for your business.

Set goals

There is no question regarding the importance of setting daily and monthly goals and targets for your company. It is also important to monitor your goals and the progress you are making. There are many business software applications that help you manage your tasks and aid in the management of your expenses and revenues.

Take pleasure in the ride

Not last, be sure to enjoy the entire process. From the very beginning of the idea until you are successful, you should be able to appreciate every step of your journey in order that in the future, you will be able to look back and be happy with what you've achieved.

Success Strategies of Successful Entrepreneurs

"To Defeat Your Competitors, Your Greatest Weapon Is Intelligence." - Sun Tzu

The majority of successful entrepreneurs we encounter these days have the same habits and methods that have made them successful. The process of starting and running a brand new venture always has an extensive learning curve, however there are certain practices that distinguish those who succeed from others. No matter how large or small you must have certain habits to ensure its efficient operation. Implementing a few good habits can be a huge boost in your venture's success.

Set realistic goals

Every entrepreneur sets his own long-term goals when they first start out. They are essential, no doubt however at the same time , it is essential to set realistic short-term goals that will help your business grow and help you build the foundation for success in the future. In the pursuit of excellence and succeed, you should not make targets that are too difficult to reach, but better still feasible and achievable. In your objectives, set ones that are simple enough to sustain you. Be aware that if over a long time, the majority of goals aren't met which can have a negative impact on the motivation levels.

Monitoring the Progress

It is essential to be aware of the short-term and long-term goals, and then see how well you're doing in reaching these goals. Make a list of audits every month and week to assess the progress made. It is also recommended to research other successful companies and their growth in the new phase.

Be mindful of the strengths you have and your weaknesses

It is essential to be aware of any advantages you might have over other companies operating in the same sector and also what distinguishes you from the rest; and strive to maximize the advantages. Additionally, knowing your own strengths could aid in better decision-making. But, knowing the positives isn't enough. You have to acknowledge your limitations and weaknesses , too and avoid taking routes that could result in more failures than gains. Once you've identified your strengths and weaknesses, you are able to hire or partner with others, or outsource to other companies who are more adept in those areas you might be weak in.

Establishing a timetable and abide to it

When entrepreneurs begin with a new venture they'll be taken in various directions. In reality, it's stated that the beginning phase is the most stressful and demanding when setting up an enterprise. In this case setting up a plan or a schedule and adhering to it is a great help. Through planning, the things that consume time are eliminated prior to the time.

Building connections and networking within your field

It is an effective method of gaining a deeper understanding and understanding of the market and start in the right direction. It is possible to gain a lot through connecting with other entrepreneurs in the same field, whether they're just beginning or established.

Learn about new trends and developments

While the majority of the learning occurs during the process of starting a business but it's always better to take part in classes or seminars that are pertinent to the company or will aid in its growth and growth. Knowing more about your business can be beneficial even if it is it is not immediately but surely in the long term.

Achieving a highly skilled workforce and directing them

In the end, every company, no matter how big or requires some extra hands to ensure it runs efficiently and grow further. At a certain point is reached, the business cannot be a one-man-show. It becomes essential to employ competent and skilled employees with the drive and drive to be the best at their job. After you have a skilled team, you must be able to be able to manage them effectively and ensure that they remain engaged and productive.

Like any other good habit, implementing these practices requires commitment and discipline. But, if you've got the desire to succeed and the drive to be the best in your ventures to become an entrepreneur Following these guidelines isn't a difficult task.

Attracting more prosperity and success

Perhaps you've noticed the importance of having a positive attitude as a business owner. It begins and ends with your attitude. This exercise will help enhance your mental health and or even boost your positive energy to gain more wealth.

You've got your objectives and aspirations, along with the determination required to attain abundance once you reach your goals right now. Until you can go through the entire law of attraction, keep an eye open.

Many successful business owners and entrepreneurs have utilized this strategy to achieve greater profits in their businesses than you'd expect.

Simple steps to reach more abundance by adopting an optimistic self-empowering mindset:

Pick a single goal to begin any of your goals with money, luxury car and growth of your business or your first dream, or any other idea to begin.

Create the most detailed images of your achievements we would like you to feel them. My family keeps a dream book filled with pictures and even drawings of our hopes and hopes.

Get your day started with your eyes fixed on the dream you're creating into your reality. If you can visualize it in your mind before you'll be able ramp up the actions required to achieve your objective.

Once you have gotten the hang of actually creating the visions of your dreams begin to affirm the goals. When you are visualizing, create an affirmation list about the goals.

Examples of affirmations I am content I'm healthy and happy, am prosperous, successful and am rich!

These affirmations should help your belief system and build on your dream. Be relaxed and don't pay attention to the events that happen, but take them as if "are"! Be confident in the reality of your thoughts and stay optimistic as you go through this method.

Another important and often neglected part of the "Law Of Attraction" is to recognize your strengths and talents already present. The feeling of gratitude is positive feeling and is the basis to trust and belief in the good things that continue to happen regardless of the obstacles you might encounter. What we think about has the greatest impact on our lives. Positive thoughts bring more good luck into your life and can boost your law of attraction required to achieve even greater success.

"When you focus your attention intently on the potential that you want to achieve and then your energy flows onto it, and draws it towards you with a force greater than the force you directed at the possibility." Stephen Richards

Friends and Family and Your Business

Take care when seeking advice on business from your relatives and friends. It's the recipe for disaster, and doesn't serve your family and friends. Do you know if a family member or friend of a member have the same business that you've started? If yes, then they are highly successful with their own company?

Ask for advice from experts on business or legal issues, particularly when you're starting or expanding your business. Be careful not to make use of family members or friends members.

I'd take it another step. If your family members provide an item that could benefit your company, pay them for their services. For instance, if that your brother is a lawyer. offer him legal advice. If your sister is a consultant for business, or a business consultant, pay her. If your friend is a business coach, make sure you pay them for their expertise.

Why should you to pay for something when you could use your relationship to obtain it for free?

If you take your work seriously, you must treat your customers with respect and professionalism in general. By valuing someone you trust enough to partner with your company, you immediately build a rapport that inspires others to be a great partner for you.

There are some who believe that you shouldn't mix family and friends with business, but my opinion is that it depends on the situation by circumstance and what is most beneficial for you, your family members and friends. Consider all the successes of "family-run" company and we could create a book focusing on only the stories of success.

We could write a book about the mishaps and disasters that were caused by people who mixed their loved ones with businesses. Personally, I love supporting my family and friends whenever the circumstances permit it. In the case of business, this could take the in the form of referrals or utilising their services. Also, it could be the times when work is put to one side and I simply enjoy the times of relaxation without the stress.

Don't forget that no company can substitute for your loyal friends and family members. The power of empowering and revitalizing the quality of your relationships outside of business can be invaluable when you are trying to get through the stressful times of growing your business.

If you do decide to use relatives and friends to aid you with your business, make sure to make sure you treat them with respect and create a an official distinction from your position as a parent or friend from that of an entrepreneurial.

"Coming together is the beginning and keeping it together is progress. Working

together is a way to achieve success."
Henry Ford. Henry Ford

Chapter 5: Start Your Startup

With all the resources and information that you require to think about, analyze and execute your venture, it's the time to start getting your business going. Based on the kind of business it can take one or two months, or years to go from the plan phase to the phase of launch. The most successful startups globally currently, invest the majority of their development phases fundraising for funds and revising the business plan. Investors who are interested in your business will be asking you questions you had not thought of, and you could need to revisit and change your business strategy. The fact that you are launching your own business shouldn't stop you from gaining knowledge about the mindset of your customers or market because it will aid in building a stronger image.

With a well-planned and upfront plan it is possible to see minimal growth and make a profit in the first couple of months following your startup's launch. These are the essential actions you should take prior to the time comes to launch your startup:

Step 1: Go over and above your plan for business

The success of launching a business is not limited to a business plan. there are many other beneficial actions you can follow. It is important to gain direct experience in the industry by learning from successful entrepreneurs. in addition, you should consider to join forces with professionals in the same business field because of their expertise and knowledge, and be prepared to test and improve your plan at every occasion. Make sure you are prepared to avoid spending too much money when setting up.

Step 2 Step #3: Try out your startup idea

You should be aware of over 50% of the new companies are unsuccessful within the first couple of years after their launch. the reason is straightforward; they jump into the launch of their business without knowing if they will succeed. Research is crucial when you are launching a new venture Make an effort to use the web and speak with real people while researching and getting the perspectives of potential customers. The best method to test your new idea is to test the idea for free in the open; this can help you to refine your idea for a startup.

Step 3: Be aware of your market

It is essential to be able to ask questions and conduct market research to find out the ins and outs in the marketplace. You must be aware of the main distributors, suppliers as well as your competition within the market you're entering. It is essential to know how much sales your rivals generate on a regular basis as well as the cost per unit that they market their products. This knowledge will not only aid you in learning how to improve your skills, but it can also help you create a long-lasting and reliable connection with potential distributors, suppliers and other market players.

Step 4: Get an excellent idea of the customers you will be selling to

Understanding more about what your potential partners' motives You must be aware of the ways they purchase their goods as well as the criteria they use when deciding on the product or service they want and the specifics about the sources of their finances and the way they use technological tools to get access to the market. If you are aware of these factors, you can figure the difference you wish to create to entice them to buy your product. You must understand the factors that influence their purchase choice, and then the best way to persuade them about the value provided by your product.

When you are in the beginning stage, you'll not have the time to make changes to your plan; hence, it is crucial to establish an appropriate plan in the beginning of your business.

Step 5: Have solid cash reserves

In the beginning of starting a new business you'll realize that you will have to invest more than you make This is why you need a reliable financial forecasting system. A cash forecasting tool is essential to ensure you can develop an outline of financial sources and backups on a regular basis. Based on your specific situation it is possible to depend on your personal capital sources, investor capital sources relatives, or even colleagues. To determine what amount of money that you'll require, create a cash flow statement in which you list your expenses as well as your income. It also means that you determine your business expenses and not just rely on estimates.

In the beginning at the beginning, you should do everything you can to reduce the requirement to use money, by avoiding long-term commitments like leasing commercial premises until there is the need for it.

Step 6: Create the correct business structure

Make sure you take advantage of the correct corporate structure for your company at the very beginning. In particular, you must to select the appropriate corporate structure when you are contemplating the legal and tax consequences of starting a new business. If you select the appropriate structure for your company and you are able to raise funds for your company soon. The right business structure will help you reduce or avoid business losses and also you'll be in a position to avoid double taxation and increase your odds of securing capital funds to grow your business in the near future.

Step 7: Start your startup

The type of business you want to start There are a variety of ways to begin your company. If you're selling products or services, you could organize an event, in which you invite the captains of industry as well as potential customers and other business stakeholders to come to the launch of your business and get an understanding of the products and services you're selling. You could also capture the event and post videos on various social media platforms such as YouTube for a boost during such an event. Make sure that your design has a distinct brand logo with a mission and identity, and should you be able to, if you wish, give away prizes or other promotional products to anyone who is present at the event.

Chapter 6: Tips To Improve Your

Credibility

Experts in marketing say that entrepreneurs can succeed or fail on the basis of their credibility. Your company might offer the top product or service anywhere in the world however if the public doesn't believe in you, your company could fail and go under.

It isn't possible to establish credibility in a hurry. Being an entrepreneur is a process that takes patience. In this section there are seven strategies to help you increase your credibility overall. Ultimately, these techniques will turn you into a successful businessman/businesswoman.

Accept Your Mistakes. Making mistakes is embarrassing, particularly when it comes to business. There are many people watching your actions: suppliers, employees customers, investors and your competition. This is that some business owners try to blame other people. This type of strategy can cause you to lose credibility. Mistakes can be embarrassing. But they can boost your credibility. It's just a matter of facing what happens to your choices.

Be sure to maintain consistency on your Social Media Sites - When it comes to establishing credibility consistent is the most important factor. You can attain consistency if each of your social media accounts have the same information. Today, consumers will communicate with your company via social media platforms.

Offer compliments. Fake compliments could damage your reputation. No one likes a smooth-talker particularly in business. However, giving a genuine and genuine compliment is a completely different story. If you praise the merits or achievements of someone, they will probably respect and appreciate your efforts.

You can offer praise to your clients, employees, customers and all others with whom you interact in your business. They will feel more confident in you in the event that they can see how much you value the work of others.

They are averse to losing - Businessmen have an insatiable determination to succeed. They seek to have ahead in nearly all negotiations. But, it's important to know that winning can sometimes damage your reputation.

Review the discussions you'll engage in for the coming days. What are you likely to risk losing? What will you gain? If you win discussions regularly could affect your personal credibility. If you are prone to twisting facts or lose your temper or lie to your opponents your credibility could be shattered to dust. It's not like you have to be a loser intentionally. It's enough to accept losses when they happen People are more likely to trust you when they are aware that you're not a sloppy loser.

Do Not Use the Word "to remain honest" There are some people who make statements by saying "to remain honest." This simple statement is subtle and can undermine its credibility for the individual who uses it. If you consider it, this statement does not really enhance the credibility of your assertions. This actually informs people that you're generally untruthful. Do you really have to tell people about your integrity? If you'd like to be credible, you must stop "being truthful."

Write articles for other sites Your credibility as a person will increase dramatically by contributing to the advancement of other individuals and groups. The task, though daunting it is actually quite simple. Contributions to the community can be made by sharing your expertise and knowledge. Nowadays, the most effective way to share knowledge and knowledge is to write articles for other websites.

If other websites publish your work, the public will be convinced of your credibility.

Do your best to win an Award Get an Award Awards provide a powerful affirmation of your abilities and credibility. They are recognized and confirmed by a third-party organisation. What can you do to get an award? It's simple: submit an application.

Most business awards aren't only given to the top people: they are sought after by those who are confident of their abilities and are willing to accept acknowledgement. But, this doesn't mean you should be overly aggressive. Be honest with yourself and determine your own strengths.

Evidently that more people will believe your abilities if you have an award that shows your abilities and reliability.

Chapter 7: Coming Up With An Idea

The best idea

There are many methods to come up with the ideal idea for your brand new venture in case you don't have an idea that you've been mulling over in your head already. The most efficient way to think of the idea is to make a list of your abilities and skills in which you excel in, as well as the things that you are enjoying in your own life. This list might be a problem-solver, adept at math writing, getting along with others, dealing with children, and the list could go without stopping.

For it to be successful your list should be derived from your heart. If you put too much thought into any particular item moment will result in a distorted picture. Also, don't try to filter your list using things you know might be lucrative (or not) The next step is later. Once you have this list completed and compiled, you can now make its opposite. The list should contain items that you can't be around and would not be able to devote the entirety of your time with regardless of the compensation. Remember, follow your instincts here and don't think too much about it.

Then, without pause to think about the suggestions you've already written down, make a list of some of the products or services that could help you in one way or the other. You can narrow your focus using these ideas since the suggestions can be attainable for a small or medium-sized company that has access to a reasonable quantity of capital.

You should ask yourself the same set of questions in relation to your professional experience, think about the things you like and dislike about your experience as well as your personal strengths and weaknesses. The final thing to think about is why you would like to begin your own business in the first place , and it is likely that there are other motives other than earning a profit.

After you've completed your lists, look at if any patterns begin to emerge. Spend some time pondering each item you found to be positive on multiple lists; there is no need to make any decisions at this point, but it's essential to allow the thoughts time to grow for you to eventually pick the most effective one.

Take a look at what you could do now: You are looking for business opportunities that you are able to take action immediately; you don't have to go back to school for more than four years to master new skills. When you are trying to narrow your list and focusing on the most popular options definitely has merit.

Finding inspiration: Creating the right business idea isn't something you'll think about on a single afternoon or evening, unless you're fortunate. You should try to keep your list at the forefront of your day-to-day routine and be aware that inspiration may come at any moment, however, you need to be ready for it. This includes being alert to the latest trends not just in your local area, but across the country too. For instance, if you are able to name a different chain of coffee establishments other than Starbucks it is that it was founded with a copycat from a nearby location into the late 90's.

This means that it is essential to not overlook tried and tested models of business because the popularity of certain niches tends to go through cycles. For instance the second quarter of 2010 has seen an growth in the popularity of gardening as a pastime and also for practical uses. Although you may not consider anything that has to do with gardening being a modern-day business There are plenty of extremely successful entrepreneurs who will argue with you. Another excellent example of this fashion is custom-made clothing. Be it cobblers, tailors, or seamstresses there is an increase in interest in clothes that are built to last.

These two examples demonstrate that you are able to take any concept and create something completely new by either updating or making a change that targets on a specific niche of market. The ability to add creativity to an existing idea isn't just an option anymore It's an absolute requirement. If your plan doesn't contain something that makes it stand out from others, you're probably losing before you even started because of the sheer amount of online competition. The only businesses that are able to operate with the same business model that works for everyone are the massive franchises. Niches are the trend of the future.

As your ideas begin to take shape The best way to be sure it's something that's worth exploring is to engage with people in your target group about the idea. This doesn't require anything formal. You do not have to divulge all the details of what makes your concept stand apart. A generalization is well. The goal is to determine the attention of those who might (theoretically) be part of the target market to determine whether you're on right path. In the process of considering all of the details can lead to getting lost in your thoughts Sharing them with someone else can help to determine if your idea has merit.

Take a look at the demand

When you have an understanding of the kind of item or service you're interested in selling then the next thing to look for is people who are interested in offering you money to purchase it. Since your concept probably came from a source from the personal, it is probably know the potential buyers for your product would be. It is important to consider this information and do studies online to find out what needs are being fulfilled today. If you've discovered an opportunity that just a tiny number of businesses are using, then great you are now prepared to move on. If not, you'll need to determine how you can modify your concept or the target market you are targeting in a manner which will enable you to make yourself known to prospective customers.

If there's only one or two businesses offering the service or product you're considering There are several reasons why this might be the scenario. The other companies and you might all be on forefront of a brand new trend, and in that case it's a good thing to have more power. If this isn't the case the reason is that the market isn't strong enough to attract significant interest right now.

To determine whether there's a gap within the market not yet filled The best method is to learn about the people who might be interested in your service or product Then, look for the websites they use. In addition to helping in the future with marketing, but it will also give you a clearer picture about the aspects of the market this segment believes are not being served. In the ideal scenario, you'll find many requests on where your particular type of service or product could be located. Even if you aren't able to discover a lot of demand for your first idea visiting these kinds of communities can be a good method to guide you in an entirely new direction.

When you are researching ensure that you visit at least eBay and Etsy because these sites are the best places to start for items that are difficult to find. These sites will instantly allow you to access an entire market which otherwise would go under the radar. If you see that interest in your product is very high on these websites, then you could consider establishing an online store in addition, provided that the competition isn't too intense.

Find out who you could meet

If you've found an item or service that has enough interest to warrant a deeper review, the next thing you should consider is the strengths of other competitors on the market. Like we said that your idea should not be completely oversaturated within the marketplace. It is important to keep competition at a an acceptable level, so that you are able to be able to learn about each one directly.

It is unlikely that you will learn anything about the inside workings of these firms, but you'll know the products they offer, their target market, their general customer's perceptions and how quickly their inventory changes and gives an overall understanding of their sales.

Go to Google and think about the primary search term or phrase that best describes your service or product. What percentage of the links in the top page connect to a site which is an expert in the product or service of your specialization? In this experiment you should consider the stronger competition you discover on the initial pages of results and the more relevant. The most undesirable thing to see at this point is an entire page that contains only two businesses, which suggests that both have excellent SEO and hold a firm grip in the marketplace. As long as there's some variety on the page there is a possibility of breaking through, however it's better to return to scratching the surface.

In the event that you locate the right amount of competition, you must look at each site with a critical focus and utilize the data you discover to draw conclusions about the type of customers that the company is targeting. Keep in mind that there's no reason why the product you offer shouldn't remain in the same place as the competition in the event that your customer base is broad enough to justify its. As a rule of thumb If you are able to spend less than 2 minutes online and you can find at least two retailers offering the same items or services to the same audience and market, then you should reconsider a few things. Before taking any drastic action but, you should make sure that your competitors are in the position of market dominance. If the consumers aren't happy with what they see and your company isn't happy, it could prosper simply by offering an alternative to the current system.

Also, look at the level of SEO competence that your competitor is displaying because there's no point to be a better alternative to the standard in the event that no one can locate any information on products or services. One of the best ways to find out how you're going to stack against is to input large search keywords into Google and then examining how often you are able to find websites that you've identified as being your competitors.

This will allow you to determine whether you'd like to enter the market, maybe more than any other. It is possible to work on the style, quality of services, prices and the products provided, but if you are operating in a small market, with a prominent brand name and a small number of customers and a limited customer base, then the stack of cards is stacked against you. It may be difficult If you've become dependent on your concept, but taking it off the table and starting again can be more pleasant than investing the time and money be disappointed when you realize that your business cannot get to the top for the general Google results.

Make an opportunity

The next step to take following deciding on your goal is clearly expressing your idea effectively with a concise pitch. You must pitch your final project numerous times before products are made or even services offered. Additionally focussing on the pitch in the short term can force you to focus on the most important aspects of your business's future with extreme accuracy to ensure that you are aware of the kind of value your prospective business can bring to the market.

The purpose of a great pitch will be:

Find the best employees

Attract investors who are interested

Attract customers

It is essential to realize that, before you think of anyone doing deal with your company, it is essential to attract their interest. The most effective pitches are 20 seconds of commercials that leave the people who listen to it with an idea about the advantages they could get from working with your business. It should be easy to understand and, more than anything other than that, specific.

Are you already thinking in your head that the strategy is too complex to be reduced to 20 seconds, why not? Try. If you feel that your idea is too complicated, you've not taken the time to clarify your concept. This is often an indication that your primary concern is how your company will make money, not whether it can add value.

There is a lot of noise in the marketplace, regardless of the type. It is essential that you practice your pitch to help you be able to cut through the majority of that noise. Making your pitch concise is essential in ensuring that you hold your audience's attention throughout. Don't talk about the history of your business in detail with no exemptions. Your message should make your audience intrigued to find out more about your company. leave the details to drinks parties.

Develop your pitch around explaining the issue that the product will solve for the audience. If, for instance, you're selling a product designed to block out the noise cats emit when walking in the street, your pitch should demonstrate that cats create loud noises right in the beginning. Once you've identified your problem then the next step is the presentation of your service or product in as to appear to be the most sensible option to link it to the problem already identified.

Explain the connection between the issue and the solution you will solve it in the most concise and intriguing way you can.

Ideally, you should include an aspect of your pitch that is so impressive that it leaves the person you're speaking to with without a choice but to follow up with questions.

Although constructing a pitch is only half the battle it has to be practiced and tuned to make it effective. It is important to practice it before the most people possible until you are able to get it right. After that the only thing left to do is make your pitch come to life.

Chapter 8: Marketing Environment

Pestle Analysis

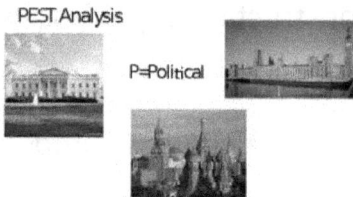

PEST Analysis

P=Political

I promised two frameworks to analyze the market environment. In the last post, we have covered SWOT analysis. The other is a PEST analysis. Sometimes, it is referred to as the PESTLE Analysis. There are six aspects to this type of analysis.

The first section of the PEST Analysis is the P for the political climate where you plan to launch your business. It is common to think it is in a stable political environment but this isn't always the case, since you are likely to launch into foreign markets that have the same political issues. Although there is some degree of security in politics within the West however, this isn't the case in other countries. If, for instance, you conduct business in African and South American countries a common issue is corruption and bribery and, in regions like the Middle East, political uncertainty. Perhaps in extreme cases however, even the possibility of national elections could have an affect your marketing decisions. Take a look at an election in Europe or presidential elections across the USA various factors that could affect where you are the best deals, and how you deal with.

2008 saw a dramatic shift in the world of finance following the collapse of banks. Before 2008 the Western global economy was flourishing and, following the crisis in the banking sector that shook the world, it sank. Before the financial crisis,, business financing was fairly accessible. Following the crisis, money became more difficult to obtain as consumer spending dropped and business growth slowed. Many businesses ended up going out of business. The ones that survived took the time to examine their expenditures, seeking ways to improve their business strategies. They took advantage of the economic climate to examine and frequently review their business practices.

While the economy is on the rise, there's never been better time to begin your own business.

We are witnessing some major changes in society, and they can impact and create new opportunities for business. There is a wave of change that is sweeping across the world of business, and has brought new kinds of business activities.

On one hand we are more connected thanks to social media, which has opened up an array of exciting commercial opportunities. On the other hand, our society is evolving, which opens up new opportunities for businesses. The social structure is changing, and in the West people are living longer, thanks to improved quality of life, hygiene and overall health. The aging population has created new markets in medical, health and spending options for the retired fairly wealthy segment.

Although they are not new, businesses are being established that exist to earn a profit however, they also give a portion of the profits back to the society for social benefit. This kind of company is referred to as a "Social Enterprise which's goal and mission is the good of the society.

Think about the present technical environment that your company is operating in. What does your service or product stand in the ever-changing technical opportunities? This is why you have determine how you intend to make use of the latest technology.

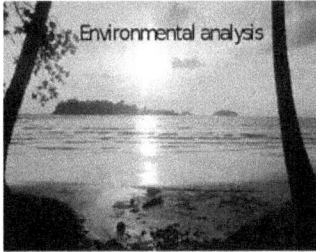
Environmental analysis

The internet offers a variety of ways to market. The book is made available as an electronic ebook with an online video course. It was traditionally been taught in a classroom , however technology offers a variety of forms and methods of delivery through online learning at any speed and at any time. Online shopping is accessible 24/7 every day of the year for trading.

Technology can open up new possibilities however, be aware and make sure to use it with care. In my international marketing venture I was able to draw a lot of attention in West Africa using Google Adwords. This technology allowed me to access these markets, however the process of converting those leads into sales was very challenging at the time. My suggestion is to concentrate on markets to which you are able to access them immediately and to be aware of the various stages of the selling process. Leads that aren't translated into sales have little significance.

PEST is able to be extended to include the letter "L" for Legal. This adds a new level of analysis. It is not a good idea to run a business without taking into account the legal framework that it has to follow.

Optional L for Legal Environment

L=Legal

Simple legal requirements could weed out early stage businesses.

The best legal compliance can be accomplished by understanding your local legislation structure. For instance in the UK you are legally able to trade as a sole trader or limited liability company. Both are beneficial and have disadvantages.

You'll need to open an account with a bank to show the legal standing of your business. There are many competing banks that can help your business , and there are many options to attract early stage entrepreneurs.

The last component that is part of this PESTLE assessment is E of environmental.

Think about the effects of environmental issues on your company and the market you're entering. In this case, we could include things as global warming, pollution, energy use recycling, and accessibility to resources that are scarce making use of environmentally friendly materials and packing.

The smart marketer will leverage these aspects to benefit through messages about eco-friendly energy, recycled products and water-saving. This aspect of the marketing environmental analysis has become more important in appealing to consumers and being part of your marketing strategy.

In the end, we have studied two kinds of tools for market analysis.

A SWOT analysis as well as A PESTLE analysis. Both are utilized to study the market. They are the tools you need to create a market entry strategy. They create a visual representation of the market you're entering. What are the things you must be aware of is the market and its conditions, that will affect your company i.e. which aspects to watch out for and capitalize on, and be aware of.

139

Activity 5

PESTLE Analysis

Your job for this part is make a fresh entry in your word doc or notebook and complete the PESTLE analysis of your current market.

Take the following as a template and then write some bullet points on each one to determine the importance to your business. It could be just an outline for now however, it will be the next step in preparing an overall business plan.

Political

Environmental

Social

Technical

Legal

Environmental

You are building the elements of a larger business plan.

Chapter 9: Skills Essential To Be A Successful Candidate For A Start-Up Position.

"The essential ingredient is getting off your back by doing something. It's as easy as that. Many people have thoughts however, there are a few that decide to take action to implement them today. Not today. Not this week. However, today."

-Nolan Bushnell, Entrepreneur

There's plenty to gain from working for a start-up however, you'll also have contribute a lot of value to the business. It is not necessary to have all of these abilities however you may want to consider a desire to enhance these skills. You may be amazed by the number of abilities you already have when you begin to consider all the things you've done and the way you achieved it.

Soft Skills

Skills in sales and persuasion

Sales are among the top soft skill you can acquire when you join a start-up any other company. The ability to sell the product, stoke the interest of prospective buyers and get them to sign up before the product has even reached the final stages of its production can be a huge help for a new business. Selling skills do not necessarily require the ability of making an offer. The skills you acquire are about the ability to be able to communicate and interact with the intended audience. Also, you must be capable of understanding the needs of the market, its wants, and issues of the particular market. This is essential for an early stage company since they put the consumer in charge to steer their product development and adapt their offerings to meet the needs of the requirements of the client. The sales skills of a startup demonstrate that you're able to invent ways to make people excited and talk about what you offer. This also means being competent in presenting the product with ease. A majority of those who are part of a startup are enthusiastic about the project they are working on , so the ability to talk about it is easy.

Communication skills

In a new company the employee is expected to participate in the team. If there is something you want to share or want to raise a problem then you must be able to express your opinion without hesitation. The ability to communicate clearly your thoughts and talk to others in the team is a talent that must be in good shape in case you want to join a startup.

Creative

Startups are known for their ingenuity and creative thinking. The most successful startups are those with an entire group of employees who come up with innovative ways to solve problems and find a novel approach for long-term success. The definition of creativity is different for everyone and that's the reason you should be open to other's perspectives, and be able to see things from a different angle. While you might be adept in figuring out creative ways to organise systems, a different member of the team might come up with a better method of enabling the team to communicate better. Together, you may develop a perfect system that increases productivity, meet deadlines within a shorter timeframe and increase the workplace camaraderie. Thinking imaginatively is also about the ability to recognize other's strengths and figuring out how to blend the two to create a more effective method to accomplish your goals.

Be part of a team and be able to work together.

Working in teams is an essential ability to be able to. It is highly likely that every person on a startup team will have a good understanding of the tasks being worked on, the deadlines and schedules, as well as the obstacles which are to be overcome. This is due to everyone being required to work in tandem. Everyone is informed of the startup's objectives and mission, so they all work together to reach the goals. Collaboration is crucial to the success of a start-up. Being able to inspire others to make use of their strengths as part of the group will result in more creative concepts.

Time management

The ability to effectively manage your time is essential when you are starting a business. Being aware of the amount of time you must devote towards each task or undertaking requires you to use your time in a efficient and efficient manner. The value of time is immense and often there isn't enough as a new business.

Organization

Although the environment at the beginning of a business may seem more chaotic than some workplaces there is always a sense of organization. The majority of start-ups operate by using simple and efficient strategies that are well-thought out and well-organized. If you don't have the ability to organize yourself and keep your focus on the task at hand or aren't aware of who to contact if you need to answer an issue or are anticipating problems, you'll soon be lost.

Corporate Skills

Problem-solving

Ability to think through problems when under pressure is crucial in working at an early stage startup. There are a variety of issues when working in at any job, but when you work for an early stage company they will face ones that do not fit into the scope of your work. It is essential to be able to tackle challenges across every aspect of the business. Because every member of the team works closely together, whatever may appear to be a concern to one person could turn into a problem for the entire team. If you don't have the capacity to tackle these issues and come up with an answer or even be component of the answer, you'll be struggling to finish your work and eventually causing massive problems and losses for the business.

The tiniest of issues won't be overlooked or not noticed. Being able to anticipate the specific problems that might be arising and then identify a solution is crucial not just to ensure your success in the beginning but also for the success of your startup in general.

Don't take it personally.

You must be able to defend yourself begin a new business the same way you would for any other corporate venture. You should be able to accept criticism and turn the criticism to benefit yourself. Also, you must be able to analyze the reason why something did not turn in the way you anticipated and determine what the issue can be, and figure out an alternative method to solve it. It is essential to be able to overcome disappointment.

Leadership. When you are a startup there are plenty of opportunities to excel in a leadership position. It could be by helping new team members, or by being the leader of the next project. It is crucial to get involved without having to wait for precise directions to be laid out for you. If you can show the manager or executive in charge that you can assume a leadership position and lead, you'll be among the first to be kept in mind when a managerial job is offered.

Technical Skills

An understanding basic of design.

Knowing how to draw a picture or design could add a lot of value to the skills you have. It is not necessary to know how to create your own designs, but you need to know what shapes are appropriate for specific colors or text to make sure you get the maximum interest. You can delve deeper into the art of design by knowing how certain designs have the ability to trigger certain emotions. You should also know ways to create a feeling of being more attracted and attracted to the style. Learn the fundamentals and develop some innovative designs and then continue to experiment every day.

Computer skills

Computer basics are something that that most people have and even in the event that you don't, not to fret because they're among the most basic skills you can acquire in a short time. You'll need to know how to control your mail account to share documents, understand the advantages of the different social media platforms as well as knowing how to conduct market research and keyword searches.

Automation

There are a variety of tools that could greatly improve workflow and enhance processes in a company. These tools are essential to a new business, and that's why knowing about these tools can be an enormous benefit. However, this doesn't mean you have to be in a position to create your own automation system. If you spot a weakness in the system of your company which could be significantly enhanced with the help of technologies that are already in place it could be the slight tweak your office may require to make for a more efficient and productive work environment.

Get a better understanding of the most well-known automation tools for business, like tools for managing projects as well as the tools for managing social media funnel system, invoice, scheduling systems and team collaboration tools. As you narrow your search for a job and locate a company that you would like to join It is important to know more about the various types of automation systems they're currently using and have more familiar with those particular tools.

Creation of content

Content creation is crucial for companies that are just striving to establish a strong brand. Although it was once a simple be a reference to written content however, now it covers various other ways to communicate information to the people you want to reach. You don't just need to be able to write long and short-form blogs as well as social media posts, but you must also understand how to create infographics videos, as well as other visual content. There's been a major shift away from written content towards visual content , such as videos since they can grab and keep the attention of viewers for longer periods of time. If you've got an knowledge of how to catch the attention of a viewer and make eye-catching graphics, it could give you an edge over those who are applying to the same position like you.

Datanalysis

Being able to evaluate the data gathered and comprehend how it impacts the performance of the business is a skill that is beneficial to possess. You should not only be able to comprehend the data you collect however, you must also be aware of the type of data is required to be gathered. Because most startups are slim and reliant on data, it is essential to collect it at all times. If you are able to demonstrate an unwavering understanding of what elements to concentrate upon based on where the company is at, this is a desired capability that every start-up requires. Additionally, being capable of identifying trends or predict expected changes in the market , and then be able to communicate them and making them clear can give you an advantage and contribute to the long-term growth of your career prospects in the startup.

Additional Skills

You must be able to rapidly adapt and take on new challenges.

The ability to adapt is essential in the world of start-ups. Things can change quickly and range from minor modifications like moving up deadlines, to more substantial modifications like completely changing the design or key aspects. Being able to adjust and progress at a the speed of light is an essential skill since day one. You'll soon find yourself being asked to take on different roles in a flash as you learn new skills in the process as well as working on your own without supervision. These situations can cause many to experience anxiety attacks, or become excessively stressed and eventually, they're tempted to quit. If you're unable to accept the inevitable and allow them to work for you, then starting a business might not be the one you'll thrive in.

Always be always curious.

The willingness to continue to grow and explore new ways of doing things is a trait that can make you a better person not only professionally, but also personally too. It could help you become an ideal employee to have to work with, which will help you secure your place in the startup firm as you've proven that you're not just willing to go above and beyond and try something new, but also aren't afraid to take on the challenges. Start-ups thrive on trying out every day new ideas and the more interested you are about taking on the obstacles and risks the better. If you're eager to discover new technologies methods, systems, or ways to approach things, it will reveal how much you're invested in continually improving your abilities in order to bring more value to your company and your position. Being open-minded and wanting to be a better learner and to take on more responsibility will allow you to make yourself a valuable resource for the business.

Be aware of your own self.

Self-awareness refers to your ability to recognize the way your actions and words affect other people. What is the significance of this? Because start-ups typically have smaller teams in the beginning and are self-aware, it is an essential ability for working as a group. If you aren't aware of that your words might be offensive to others or your actions could be a distraction to others, you'll find it difficult to collaborate within a group. The inability to be conscious of your behaviours and actions might seem like something that everyone might have, but it is frequently ignored. It is important to strike the right balance between working in a group while also being confident enough to speak your personal opinions and ideas without being a critic of the opinions of others.

Do something.

The most successful startups are ones that have grown out of employees who simply say that they've got an idea. The team then weighs the advantages and disadvantages and comes up with ways to measure the outcomes, and then tests the idea. Being able to communicate your thoughts and implement them could be a significant influence on the business. Start-ups thrive under these conditions. Sometimes, this means having to make decisions by yourself. If you've got an improved method of doing something, you shouldn't be expecting others to jump in and offer to take it on. You must be prepared to take the action to increase the value of the group.

Chapter 10: Value Of A Business

Plan

The process of creating the business plan is among the most effective opportunities to make the most of your time. The business plan will provide an exact description of your company for prospective financiers, sponsors or mentors, as well as other partners. It will help you to keep your business from drifting off course, and will aid in managing the expansion and maintain the financial viability of your company over the long term.

A business's plan of action is a formal document that details your business plan for every major aspect that you operate in. It lists the goals of your business and marketing strategies as well as your budgetary plans. For all practical goals, it's your business, and especially prior to when your daily operations begin.

A business plan could aid in obtaining loans from banks and other investors.

Without a fully-fledged business plan, no one will think of investing in your company. Potential supporters and partners will want to read your business plan prior to committing to backing your venture.

As your business grows, your business strategy will evolve. It's a document that's constantly evolving as that you modify as your company changes to reflect the changing needs of the market. It will be referred to it when you lead your company along the course you've laid out for your business. A business plan could be the difference between success in business and utter failure.

While some entrepreneurs employ an outside writer to assist create their business plans It is actually quite simple to write your own. The following description will help you through this processby giving you an overview of each part of your business plan.

The Executive Summary

An average business planning has nine parts, starting with an executive summary. This will comprise around 10 percent of the overall plan, and will provide a concise description of the details that follow. Many potential investors are only interested in this portion and it is crucial to ensure that your summary is written well. Your readers should know quickly and clearly the fact that you have an excellent business concept, waiting to come to life!

A lot of entrepreneurs draft their executive summary in the last minute. Once you've fought to convey the information clearly you will find it easier to write an outline that covers the fundamentals of your company as they're fresh in your thoughts. If you're looking to use the summary an outline of the main points you want to write about later on I suggest that you go back to the summary once you've finished. Sometimes , things shift in the process of supplying the specifics, and you'll need to ensure that the summary still represents the truth of the other elements part of the business strategy.

A summary of executive should introduce your audience of choice and provide an effective argument to explain the benefit that your company plans to provide the audience. In addition you must clearly define the way your company plans to present its services and products available to the audience you intend to target.

In addition, you should explain in your summaries the ways your business can be different from the rest of the competition. It should include a convincing and realistic three-year financial projection to show that your company deserves the reader's support. In addition, you should outline the team you have assembled and your launch strategy.

Description of the Startup

This is where you are able to go into the intricacies of your company. Your startup's description must include your company's name, the legal form and the location you're planning to establish, as well as your personal story, such as the reason you got the idea in the first place.

The section also includes your mission statement as well as the vision statement of your startup. The mission statement outlines the the values of your business and clearly explains where your company is heading. The vision statement is a concise outline of how you will define the success of your venture, as well as the potential growth you anticipate in the initial few years.

In line with your vision and mission statements, you must briefly rephrase your product's outline and reiterate the definition of your customers. The startup description should conclude by presenting goals for your business. These are the main goals that you've established for your startup in the course of doing your market and industry study.

and Services. and Services

This is where you are able to give a thorough overview of the items you'll be selling. The most important thing is to explain the way your products are different from the ones sold by your competitors. If your primary selling point is a tangible item make sure you provide a photo-like description of the details. Make sure to clearly describe the physical characteristics and unique attributes, as well as why it is unique to the target market. Be sure to back up your claims by presenting the findings of your market research . Also, explain how you'll meet the anticipated demand, and the resources utilized to achieve this degree of production.

Market Outlook And Market Analysis

You're likely to be familiar with the profile of the industry from a few chapters ago. It is easy to look up the information that you've gathered and put it together into a concise report in this section. The purpose behind the information you provide is to convince investors that your business is worth their money. The best approach is to blend your market analysis with research that focuses on the purchasing habits of your customers. You can then include it in your startup's budget initial.

Decribing Your Operations

In addition to your industry outlook, an analysis of the market is the part that focuses on the operations of your business. Smaller businesses can benefit by listing all the things they've done to date in terms of their operations (e. such as. renting office space or purchasing supplies). This is a place where you'll need to keep track of regularly when your company grows and your operations get more complicated.

It is important to provide a description of the production procedure. For instance, if opening an establishment for bakery, you can detail the type and the quantity of materials you'll require for the production of your bakery's line of baked goods. You should also identify the people who will be producing these products, and how. If you're operating out of a physical location it is important to provide the hours of your storefront along with your address, as well as any other details that relate to the physical operation of your business.

This is also the area to describe your quality assurance procedures as well as the specifics of your supplier relations.

Management Team

The section must include details about the hiring process, as well as an overview of your managerial structure. If you are a member of an advisory board it is the right area to provide information about the current and planned composition of the advisory board.

Establishing an advisory committee shows that you're committed to launching your business. If you include this information in your business plan, you show that you're willing to consider the advice of others as you move forward in your venture. Members of the advisory board are usually experts with years of experience in the world of business and bring specific experience in the room. Your advisory board meets frequently to discuss the most important aspects of your company.

Examining Your Competitors

A competitor analysis is a good way to keep track of market trends and explain to investors how you will tackle the challenges. Your direct competitions are companies that offer the same or similar product as yours. A thorough analysis of your competitors includes a detailed description of their particular strengths and weaknesses compared in comparison to your own strengths and weaknesses, a review between the efficacy of your different areas, an evaluation of your intended audiences as well as an evaluation of your marketing strategies, a review of your growth forecasts along with a description of opportunities that your competition missed that you intend to utilize to your advantage. It's also helpful to include an analysis of SWOT (as as described in the chapter on SWOT) in this part of your strategy.

Marketing Strategy

The following section will be the method you select to promote your product and services intended public in the most effective manner that is possible. The main goal of this plan is to promote your product in a way that you'll be able to make money without spending a fortune. Marketing can be expensive and the proper strategy can increase sales while preserving your margin of profit.

The marketing plan you create will outline your target market, presenting an accurate image of your ideal customer. It is followed by an outline of the analysis you conducted on the marketing strategies of your competitors. Then, you provide a thorough review of the method you'll employ to stand out from your competitors. Your marketing plan should include the details of your budget for marketing the strategy you will use to market and establish your brand, the way you intend to use strategic pricing strategies and how you plan to efficiently distribute your product and it will conclude with a thorough outline of your marketing platform.

Financial Plan

The financial plan outlines how you plan to manage your finances, while balancing costs and profits. It combines the different figures pertaining to your company to outline how you plan to lead your new venture through its early years. It describes how you will to manage all the aspects in such a way to ensure that your business is financially stable as you build your business up and running.

The three main components of this section include your profits and losses statements and balance sheet as well as your report on cash flows. Together, these documents give an accurate view of the financial situation of your company. Starting with the current situation and extending to the place your company would be six and twelve months, followed by the two- and three year period.

Since the beginning of a startup is essentially information Your business plan should comprise an estimate of sales that outlines the numbers that you think your business will produce over the three years to come. Of course, you'll provide the reasons of your numbers in explaining how you arrived at these numbers.

A much simpler way to determine is an outline of your business's expenses. If you can list the anticipated expenses, you will be able to easily come up with a reasonable business budget that can assist you in managing your finances from the start and also plan to pay for these expenses using profits.

Write Your Business Plan

If you're not sure about certain terms or strategies I've discussed in this book, don't worry, this is what the rest of the book will cover. When you've read through the chapters you'll be able to complete the specifics of what I've sketched out. A great business plan shouldn't be too elaborate. It's just important to clearly define your plan of action and be written in a manner to be read by the common person.

Conclusion

We thank you for reading this book. In the first chapter of the book, we said that we would that we would show you how to create a genuine coaching business, one which isn't just an occupation where you exchange hours in exchange for dollars.

We began by discussing the difference between the two. A job is one in which you are paid an hourly wage. We talked about what you should do to be aware of in order to avoid it.

A lot of people believe that they require credentials or experience to be an instructor. We've examined this issue in detail.

Then we looked into the subject of money. Are you able to be an instructor for someone who earns more money as you? If so, what are the advantages your skills bring? And how do you make it work?

Every successful coach is known by their name. They are sought-after by people who are eager to work with them due to the good reputation they have earned for their coaches. Reputation was at the heart of the chapter that followed the book.

Then we have discussed the products you're selling when you are an online coach. We also discussed the subject of controlling clients as well as the best way to charge for your coaching services for an on-line coach.